Surviving Home

Surviving Home

Poems by

Katerina Canyon

© 2021 Katerina Canyon. All rights reserved.
This material may not be reproduced in any form,
published, reprinted, recorded, performed, broadcast,
rewritten or redistributed without
the explicit permission of Katerina Canyon.
All such actions are strictly prohibited by law.

Cover design by Shay Culligan

ISBN: 978-1-63980-001-8

Kelsay Books
502 South 1040 East, A-119
American Fork, Utah, 84003
Kelsaybooks.com

To Mozell,
The screaming boy in the closet

Acknowledgments

Thank you to the editors of the following journals and anthologies for publishing these poems in their earlier forms:

Black Napkin Press: "Creating Zeus"

CatheXis: "Penance"

Daffodils: "A Petition for Unrecognized Children," "Wingless Dreamer"

Esthetic Apostle: "Skill"

Into the Void: "Follow the crack pipe"

Meniscus: "Aunt May," "Quintessential Pirate"

Our Story—From Harriet to Kamala: An Anthology of Black Women Poets in Tribute to Black Women Firsts: "Sojourner"

The Write Launch: "House at Night," "My Life Map"

Twyckenham Notes: "After Landing in Lisbon"

Waxing & Waning: "At 13, I found a bra," "I Am the Complete Secret"

Thank you to the following books and poets who inspired this work:

Mai Der Vang, *Afterland*

Catherine Barnett, *Human Hours*

Mahmoud Darwish, *I Don't Want This Poem to End*

For their generosity, talent, and friendship, a special thank you to Danny Bryant, Madonna Bryant, Aja Minson, James Trueblood, Rachel Reyes, Coco, Asia Renee, Kelli Russell Agodon, Katy Didden, Devin Johnston, Don Campbell, Rick Lupert, Sharon Smith-Knight, Eileen Carole, Mary Bast, Adrienne Klein, Rachael Levy, Susan Dax, Wanda Parks, James Evert Jones, and Michelle Richards-Haug.

My dearest thanks my brothers for allowing me to share a piece of them in these poems. There would be no poetry without them.

Thank you to Karen Kelsay and Delisa for having faith in my work.

Thank you to my publicist Kelsey Butts for working so hard to let the world know about this book.

Thank you to my husband Geoff who sat with me every day in the hospital while I recovered. Thank you to my children who constantly give me a reason to smile, laugh, and live.

Contents

Involuntary Endurance	13
I Wish I Could Tell You This Has a Happy Ending	15
Surviving Home	16
I Say You Can't Go Home Again	18
I Felt My Brother's Wrists	22
Thoracic Biology	23
My Pain Is Sculpted into Art for You to Consume	25
My Life Map	27
Skill	29
Small Bear to Great Bear	31
Playing with Roses	33
An Afterthought of a Netflix Show	35
The Tyger, Interrupted	37
The New Hope	39
At 13, I Found a Bra	40
Authority Questions	41
The Last Lecture	42
Trifling with Heroin	43
Aunt May	45
All Day Long	47
Bessie's Reincarnation	50
Holding Still	51
House at Night	52
Blessings	53
Fan	55
In Consideration of the Black Bear	56
Child Bride	57
A Die Cast on Sand	58
Silver Sunrise	59
Scrabble	60
Before God	61
Creating Zeus	62

Celestial Messenger	63
Witness	64
Freedom from Speech	65
A Petition for Unrecognized Children	67
Sojourner	69
Donald Trump Is My Father	71
I Left Out "Bells and Whistles" Written with a Little ___Help from Websters Dictionary	73
Secrets	77
A Plea to the Inane	79
My Guardian Angel	80
Phoenix	81
Penance	82
I Stop Praying When I Learn You Abandoned Me	84
While Dreaming of Harvey Weinstein	86
Yet Another Attempt at Self-Immolation	89
Follow the crack pipe	91
No More Poems About My Father	93
Partial Aphorism	94
NYP Psychiatry	95
After Landing in Lisbon	97
Quintessential Pirate	99
I Am the Complete Secret	101
Censorship	103
Epilogue	105

Involuntary Endurance

My story is not one revealed with chapter
And verse. It is expressed in blood and bone.
It is fingernails thrust into back muscles.
It is razorblades pressed against flesh.

It is told by how the shark swims
Through the ocean—below a school
Of tuna, and it is not the shark's story.
It is the school of tuna searching along

The vast dark but sunlight-speckled ocean
While knowing they have everywhere
And nowhere in the world to flee.

It is the brown bear pulling honey
From the honey-comb in order to
Teach her cubs to survive on their own.

It is not the mother bear's story.
It belongs to the cubs who wander
The forest without her after she sacrificed
Her life to a boar grizzly to protect them.

It is told through hot cylinders of pain
That sear experience into the skin.

It is told in front of the sharp bayonet
That sprays blood-red existence against
The multi-colored palette of the universe.

It may sit silent and still
On these black and white pages,
But it exists in every tremble
Of my leathered hand, and it is smeared
Into every tear-stained scream
that flows through my quavering pen.

I Wish I Could Tell You This Has a Happy Ending

I held the knife in my hand
I propped open the blade
I sharpened it against petrified wood
But I could not slice my flesh.

It was not that I fear the pain
Or the blood
I'm familiar with both
I am a woman after all.

The world blinds me with its
Whiteness. I must pretend
Happiness exists when
I can see nothing.

I don't know if there will be
Morning. I have already
Pondered chasing the seagulls
From my balcony

I have no trust in humanity
I lost that when I was 3
It was baked in a pan of
Cornbread and eaten by

Demons. Life is a gift I cannot
Seem to appreciate right
Now but I will try to make it
Through the night—help me!

Surviving Home

My father is a shark
with a hope chest
clenched between his teeth.

It holds my brain
and heart perfectly.

Earthquakes rumble.

A castle crumbles
into the water.

The sea is filled with bones.
I tread water. Pulled away
by a tsunami.

The boat in the distance is a crypt.

The ocean foams blood.
The buoys sink. They leave me
wondering where to go.

My lungs maintain
because I come from
light and air.

The mermaid is a woman
made of music and desperation.

I put my ear
against her chest, and I hear
her dreams.

A million notes coat my skin,
and I float above the storm.

I Say You Can't Go Home Again

During the time immediately
after homelessness and shortly
preceding hopelessness
we squatted in a dispossessed
house in Perris, California

This is where she created gardens
from clippings of other roses
she stole from neighbors' front yards.

Sometimes, she'd ask
but most times
she would sneak up to a bush
pull clippers out of her bag
snip off a branch and hurry away

a rose petal shoplifter

She grew at least twenty varieties
white, black, yellow, orange,
spots, trims, mixtures,
and of course
red

This is where the owner was busted
for selling and manufacturing PCP and
this is why all the doors
except the front
were off their hinges

And this is why we were
living in a four bedroom ranch
house on five acres with a pool

This is why the small guest house out
back smelled like a combination of
gasoline, nail polish, and molasses

This is where we threw garbage because
we couldn't afford a trash fee

This is where
we found the dogs
the police shot
parched dead
intertwined
with tumbleweeds

This is where he made us dig
because he knew there were
gallons of PCP buried somewhere
in the five acre yard

This is where he would sit
in his lawn chair and shout
instructions to us with promises
of sharing the wealth if we found it

Our own toxic liquid treasure hunt

This is where he handcuffed him
well into the night

He would come out periodically
and beat him with a bullwhip
because he was caught shoplifting

It was not the crime itself that
bothered him because they would
shoplift together

It was the getting caught
that was the punishable offense

This is where we would heat the water
for baths, dishes, and laundry

It took hours to get things done

we had to scrub laundry
on a washboard and
hang it to dry

The year was 1983

This is the walkthrough closet that
connected me to them and all
their conversations and the radio

I often heard Paul Harvey say "Good Day"

This is the way he used
to sneak into my bedroom

This is the bed I used to sit on
as I tried to figure a way out

This is the window I stared out
when I felt trapped

This is where the roses used to be

Tracing a path along the driveway
to the back where she kept the bed
with all her favorites

I Felt My Brother's Wrists

Bound around a phone pole
By handcuffs in the dark
Desert night. I heard
His screams and the whip's crack.
Like thunder following lightning.

He was thirteen, I think. I was
Fifteen, maybe. That time sits in a cloud
Without minutes. I just remember
Twitching as if each crack were
Against my back.

But they were not. I am just a witness.
I hover through storms and report
The heat index of memories.
That night, the sky was crimson.

The moon shined like a spotlight
Against atrocities. The whip stopped
When the screams stopped.
Then my father left him standing

And bound to the pole
For the rest of the night.

Thoracic Biology

For the most part I want to learn to let go,
to hurt a little less.
My heart is what hurts the most.

Where did I learn to
breathe through the pain, to
cut off the sword piercing through

my left lung?
I think it was the woman who taught
me to read, who taught me
to understand language,

or maybe it was the man who
pressed the hot scalpel of innuendo
against my skin?

The chambers of the heart are
maidenheads. Getting through
is what I consider making love.

Not that I have had many
lovers, more through my head than my heart.
Last night I dreamed of sex in a

bed made of quicksand, where I
furrowed and sank in undulating beats.
I loved the way I was surrounded

by obsidian, the heat, the magma
that ran through my aortic arch,
the holding on, the seizing, the pain.

Most times, when I sleep, I dream of
my hands, clutched tight around something
I cannot see, and I cannot let go.

My Pain Is Sculpted into Art for You to Consume

Here is my pain
Gunshots echoing into the night
Bullets whizzing past me
As I flee across abandoned lots.
Heroin hidden behind the pink bow in my panties.
Consume it.

Here is my pain.
Switch marked whooppin's.
The smell of PCP.
A black man dead in a Texas creek.
Consume it.

This is my pain.
My mother beaten black by my father.
My father beaten blue by police
Over my voice.
Consume it.

This is my pain.
My furniture pushed past the sidewalk
While L.A. Marshals watched
And my friends stared.
Consume it.

This is my pain.
Getting stopped by police
For mumbling reasons.
Getting searched without cause.
Being followed in fear.
Consume it.

This is my pain.
Watching my black mother die
While watching white women live
With the same thing.

Seeing my tiny baby thrive among
Fat white babies.
Consume it.

This is my pain.
Watching black babies die.
Consume it.

This is my pain.
Watching black boys die.
Consume it.

This is my pain.
Watching black men die.
Consume it.

Discuss it.
Write it.

Allow it to give you verbal diarrhea
On CNN, MSNBC and FOX news.
Give it a BlackLivesMatter hashtag

Then do absolutely nothing.

My Life Map

The portrait of my childhood
resides in Thomas Brothers' Guides

My home is carpeted in asphalt
and built with median walls

Take the 110, exit Slauson
to my birthplace

Head south on Vermont
and right on Manchester
for my elementary school

Imperial Highway to Dockweiler
Daily vacations and to watch
Dad drink wine and smoke weed

91 East to high school
91 West to leave high school

Park on Manchester and Prairie
to go to the track

Live at the motel across the way

Dad called me a whore on the sidewalk

Take El Segundo to Willowbrook
for Mom and Dad's heroin

Take Manchester again for SSI checks

Go up LaBrea for Dad's Sherms

Sleep in the car on Rosecrans

Off Century and Alameda to find Dad's crack

Near LaCienega watch cancer eat away at Mom slowly

Sleep on the streets downtown on 7th

South on 405 to start over

Skill

Her stained hands wear beet juice like blood
as her dark fingers glide
the thin silver steel blade around
one cardinal globe after another

It is difficult to distinguish the difference
between skin and flesh

but she does it adeptly

I ask, *how can you do that so easily?*

She responds, *I just do*

Husks break free
and blotch the butcher block crimson

I ask,
doesn't it scare you to use something so big?

No
she responds

Her large butcher knife hovers
and dances over the submissive orb
as it turns

I ask, *what's a period?*

She nicks her finger
winces, drops the beet
and grabs a towel

I tell her,
you should use a peeler

She says, *it's a sorry
tool that blames its master*

I reply,
I think you got that backwards

She slams the knife on the board
and with a quick flash of turning tide,
she looks me in the eye and
says
Girl, you know what I mean

I look down quickly
pick up a beet peel
and dye my fingertips red

Small Bear to Great Bear

"There's the big dipper" I say
"No" she splays my
fingers into fronds
and measures
the night sky
from minor to major

"There's the big dipper"
she corrects

"They are all the same"
I say

She replies "No—they all have their
place—their color—like race
you cannot move
from one to the other"

I dismiss their distinctive twinkles
and say "they are the same"

"They're not" she denies
"They are in different places
Like you and me"

"But we're both here"
I—
Her hands rise
before my face
and blocks the
stars before my eyes

"No—We're not"
"You're here
I'm back there"

Playing with Roses

I dropped petals from the
      stem like confetti

          He loves
          He loves me not
          He loves me

You often
picked up roses by the thorns
without piercing your skin

A gentle grasp
from bush to vase

Now I have no roses
No velvet kisses
on my finger tips

The last blossom
died with you

A hostile desert
inhabits my hands

Your talent resides
somewhere within me

Memory is enough
to make it bloom

You showed me
      roses every day

Pressed in my palms
Thorns pierced my skin

We are daughter and mother
Bound by the same sanguine root

        She loves me
        She loved me
        She loves me

An Afterthought of a Netflix Show

When my mother was in college,
one of her professors said
she looked like a black Carol Burnett.

It has been 31 years since my mother's death,
and I still search Carol Burnett shows
for traces of her within Carol's face—

eyes gray, not brown—
hair red, not brunette.
I merely see mist.

My mother lived with a man who abused her
every day. She said there was nowhere to go.
She died before I hit 20.

When I grew up, I lived with a man
who abused me every day.
Carol said, "Only I can change my life.

No one can do it for me," so I left
with bruises on my neck, and a baby
at my waist. At least Carol endures with me.

She is five years older than my mom,
if my mom had lived.

I am one year older than my mother ever lived.

It feels wrong passing my mother. It is as if
I have been caught at six years old
wearing her favorite dress, shoes, and perfume.

Carol looks pretty good for her age.
Her hair is still red.

I'm sure it is dyed—when my mother died,
she was mostly gray. I am not,
but I have less hair than she did.

Right now, you can watch Carol Burnett on Netflix.
I don't think she will get a second season.

It seems like "stay woke" doesn't
carry the same cache as "so long."

In the end, I prefer to watch reruns.
They sit on my mind like happy memories,
of which I have so few.

Most of my flashes of the past are visions of beasts.
I wish I could spend the day watching Carol talk
to children, but alas, I have grown-up things to do.

The Tyger, Interrupted

And with all due appreciation to William Blake

Tyger Tyger, burning bright,
In the forests of the night;
What immortal hand or eye,
Could frame thy fearful symmetry?

Girl, stop reading and clean this sink.

In what distant deeps or skies.
Burnt the fire of thine eyes?

Girl stop reading, or I'll knock you
Into next week!

On what wings dare he aspire?
What the hand, dare seize the fire?

How (*smack*) many (*smack*) times (*smack*)
Do (*smack*) I (*smack*) have (*smack*)
To (*smack*) tell (*smack*) you?! (*smack*)

And what shoulder, & what art,
Could twist the sinews of thy heart?
And when thy heart began to beat,
What dread hand? & what dread feet?

Girl!
Stop reading.
Run to the store and fetch me some cigarettes.

What the hammer? what the chain,
In what furnace was thy brain?
What the anvil? what dread grasp,
Dare its deadly terrors clasp!

Girl, stop reading. Now just hold it
at the base—like that.

When the stars threw down their spears
And water'd heaven with their tears:
Did he smile his work to see?

Girl stop reading and come clean these collard greens.

Did he who made the Lamb make thee?

Tyger Tyger burning bright,

Girl, Stop reading & take this trash outside

In the forests of the night:
What immortal hand or eye,
Dare frame thy fearful symmetry?

Girl—Stop reading.

The New Hope

Sitting atop the wall
In my backyard, sitting
Out the broadcasts of draft notices on t.v.
Maybe the wall will hold
My brother away from Vietnam.

Sitting atop the cement block wall,
Kicking loose dirt from my Mary Janes,
Ants scramble beneath showers of dust.
Life and death separate between
Blades of grass.

I am balancing atop a telephone wire
Between tossed sneakers
And lost kites and crows' caws.
Atop my head sits a squirrel,
And in my mouth, blindness replaces sight.
Where the sun freezes in my hand,
And the moon burns my eyes,
And I kick away the crust between my soles,
This is where I will find a picket fence
Painted white like dandelions.

At 13, I Found a Bra

I had not prayed for the monsoons
reveling between my breasts.

The bullfrog that beats beneath
my pectoral muscle

cannot fit into a second-hand mold.

Along my Sierras grows an
    orchard of knowledge of good
    and evil. I take my beatings. I
    bind myself in woman's hood.

I hook the clasps
along my curved spine.
Only the band knows
the stress of my heart.

I am told every woman
pays her debt with pain.

    When the daffodil opens,
    the last breath of childhood releases.

I already knew
long before he
called me a whore
where I stood
in his bloodshot mind
before his crooked eyes.

I am the harlot—
Christ's final temptation,
binding the mind to cause.

Authority Questions

Would it have been different
if I were white, and if I had blue eyes,
and I lived on a ranch with 500 head of cattle?

Would the doctor have still called me a liar?
Which he did. Would he have made the nurses
hold me down while he pushed the speculum inside me?

Would he have said, "There are no black virgins
living in the Midway" before he found my hymen?
Which he did. Before he called my mother?

Which he did. Before he was proven wrong?
Which he was.
Would I have told my mother

if my father hadn't already taught me
how to be a good girl,
how to be quiet,

how to use the workarounds and hold on to virginity?

Would I still have something to give…
Innocence…Love…Trust…
if it had not been taken from me already?

The Last Lecture

За Здоровов mumbles the pill
Beneath my tongue
As I press it against my teeth.

Life is a plum, moans mama's ghost,
Stolen from between the lips
Of an absent schoolgirl.

Life is a vulture, sighs papa's succubus.
Brilliant. Rampant. Extravagant. Sharp.
It will catch you while you sleep.

Whenever you are lost,
It will find you. My daughter,
Remember your lessons.

Diagram. Box of bones!
Dark circles, sallow skin.
The first taste is free.

My tribe is cloying
Within my stomach.
Make sure to set them loose

Before you go.

Trifling with Heroin

She learned to cut lines at eight

> *Look at her*
> *She's so cute*
> *She's imitating me*

So proud
To see the girl playing with salt

She slowly scraped
A playing card

Along the dark wood
Catching every grain

The transition to heroin
Was a given

The wife's little helper

Antipathy grew
From heroin, to PCP, to crack

You often accused her
Of stealing—being against you

Stillness was threatening enough

You played this game
Day-to-day

Joined by no one
Separated by futile talents

This is your daughter
Sitting at your knee

> *Now cut more*
> *Into the other line*
> *Make them straight*

Aunt May

She cries at the stereo as if
it could take her to heaven on the
notes of Z.Z. Hill's *Down Home
Blues,* every other record or two.

Uncle L. Joe, *that no good
son of a bitch* held her heart in a vice.

Then he died, relegating him to the
beloved angel he never was, fleeing into

mangled clouds, on shredded wings, made of
brambles, as if Texas soil were fertile. Hill's
throat pulls notes—his voice trickling crude into
Aunt May's Los Angeles living room.

Z.Z. Hill is redemption coated in Texas blood.

L. and Z.Z. are one. Their crooning calls
to her before the song ends, and she restarts.

Their voices harmonize mercurial,
chaotic as oil gushers
spilling into the fields of Canaan. In

The Promised Land, there are no negro
spirituals, no blues

no white man's hand smiting the black man's face,
but there is always a burden for the black woman.

She knows this song well, and she plays it again.

Down Home Blues, Down Home Blues
Every other record or two.

All Day Long

In a few minutes, my father will toss the
Screaming boy into the closet.
I will be sent in behind him,

As a sedative, the autism whisperer
In knee socks and a snoopy tee shirt.

I was always able to contain the
       Rabbit, having once been a
              Rabbit myself,

Before my birth,
And I recall the transition,
       The piercing of the coral shell,

The faucet that opened and the hook
That broke my character.

I should have held tight to
             My mother's twine.
My lock should have tied true.

Instead, my framework is cracked.
       I cannot repair it with plaster or
     Denial, and truth does not burnish it either.

I hold my brother's hand.
I clench my breath.
His scream lowers to a bleat.

       The closed door becomes an ocean,
       Our prison an oasis.

Just he, me, and the sea

Playing hand-clap games,

And we cannot be bound.
        We are free, I tell him.

              We are infinite
Because I declare it
As sister and deity.

Our situation is what it is: We are stuck.
We can choose whether we are stuck
In darkness or in light.

You can find both truth and lies
In perception.
Does he understand me?

Autism makes him mute not stupid.
We are free. He laughs.

        We are free. I laugh.
        We are free as we clap
        Our hands together

And laugh and I sing songs
Of birds tweeting and razz a matazz,

While he claps, and sways, and
He rocks back and forth.
His bleat is a hum.

Perhaps that was he,
Or maybe it was I

Who had the rabbit's scream.
Who's to remember?

Bessie's Reincarnation

I long ago toted my Mastodon life
In a large green Glad bag.

Sidewalks—my trusted friends
Protected me away from home.

Guided by street lamps
Daylight never left. I rarely

Slept in the skyscraper's shadow
When my eyes shut. The song of

Traffic electrified my mind
Dancing throughout rush hour.

Fires burned in tar coated oil drums. Here I
Separated myself from sleeping bags

Lying side-by-side on 6th. Tombstones
Holding specters in my eyes.

Holding Still

I once lived in a gorse covered cage
buried deep beneath the Aqueduct.

Impenetrable to water
I survived on flames
sparked over apocalyptic amethysts.
Smoke never escaped. I held

the purple embers between my fingers
to frighten the bats.
If I clenched my fists
as my mother taught me,

I could see the sunrise
100 years away.

Each night before I imagined sleep

legs crossed, I inhaled
incandescence
and breathed out rain.

House at Night

Gold-flecked dust ignites in waves.
I kiss my desert skin.

The coyote's song lulls me
before I count the sheep.

The doorknob will turn
       before the lock's clasp

protects me from
       what is inside.

****

Numb as a tortoise
who hides in his shell,

I take the bite of the rattlesnake
who breaks his fangs on my carapace.

I swallow the venom from his lips.
I consume his allotrope skin,

take in the flesh as taffy
       between my teeth.

****

He dies as I play
       his song,
"Papa was a Rolling Stone."
The notes are tucked into a journal.
My cracked voice sings,

When he died,
       all he left me
              was alone.

Blessings

It's a far cry
        from shoeless.

Buster Brown patent leather shoes
        with bows while toes
        are squeezed in tightly

to fit.

It's a far cry
        from starving.

Banana and Sunny D in the morning
        free lunch at school
        beans and rice for dinner.

Sometimes nothing.

It's a far cry
        from homeless—

An abandoned house
        in the middle of nowhere
        with doors propped up

with two by fours.

It's a far cry
        from rape—

The acts he makes
        you perform
        so close your eyes and

think of pretty things.

It's a far cry
        from over—

This life you live,
        so take time to hope
        for snow in the morning

fireflies at night
and Thrifty's ice cream
in the afternoon.

Fan

On her knees, with a buttoned
grin, she presses her auburn chin
against the silver steel grate.

She wills cool air from
humidity, which flies between
brisk blades and resides

upon her cheek. In her
ears she catches the drum
of the motor, and her

teeth hum like drunken bees.
She shuts her eyes before
they dry and dreams

of snow, of wind, of icy
sheets of rain. Her
hair stands straight

in static shock as she smacks
her nose against the blades.
She stands and takes

two steps back, and two
steps back until all she
feels is heat and pain.

In Consideration of the Black Bear

Butterfly wings are tidal waves
Sunrise's gulls are diving
for the last moonlight

Most dreams evaporated in the frying pan

You and I come together in a hen's egg

By the end
        we will sing negro spirituals

Dance our eyes
        atop the Cuyamacas

I will taste your branches
        as they rest against the fence

Every leaf is a nest
        Each seed—a galaxy
                dropping between blades of grass

I was raised to be
        the perfect fault—
                to take the blame

        to allow you to be King

Child Bride

I wish for an innocent childhood
With wide-eyes I wish
I wish for dolls with curls
I wish for a frilly satin dress
With a few puffy bows
I wish for the soft embrace of my mother
I wish for cartoons on Saturday mornings
And laughter during hopscotch
In the afternoon
I wish for ice cream
Melting over my tongue
I hope for a lovely prince
Who can rescue me like a lost kitten
I wish for a feathery life
I wish for a great deal
I do!

A Die Cast on Sand

I thought your hard edges
were stone and immovable.
Your freckles change

all minds depending on the side
you show
        fortune or destruction.

When I rolled you over
and your character changed
as you were nestled in dust

spread before oceans of fire
akin to a volcano, ashen ore,
        acrimony,

your disregard fought with a wishbone.
You gave me your heretic,
cornerstone speech, metamorphic rock

ground into gravel and grit.
After sunset, you showed me
        revelations of rubble

buried in my fragmented shell.
I held you. You did not move,
yet my heart did.

When waves buried you beneath the water
I reached into the seaweed
        and plucked you out.

Silver Sunrise

Rain, then flood
then garbage.

White plastic bags
float atop the marina

like bleached seal
bellies.

A whale coasts
down the channel
with no way out.

Seagulls sort through
cigarettes on the sand.

Thin seashells
split my fingertips.

Pelicans dive into the surf
and come up empty.

Tiny crabs skitter along the beach
to hide in air bubbles

Dolphins rise from the sea
heading north.

Sea monsters
roll in with the
tide and die
on the sand.

Scrabble

It is just one word. We count the tiles
on our stands, a medley of wooden squares.

Changing them from a jumble of nothing
words, construct our poetry to the canvas.

Charge the pencil to the score pad, and our
scores are the codex. Some letters are

worth more than others. Some words
worthless, as the tiles reveal.

Inscribe our minds like chalk. Hopscotch
of a child's dance. Qi, quiets, quits.

When it's over, I'm left with a blank.

Before God

You were crushed into me.
    Through stone and pestle, he pressed
thistle and thorn
    (the Creation).

You came the seventh day
    to take my milk and innocence.
Together we
    rested against
        sage and tumbleweeds.

When you cried, I nursed
    you in bitter milk.
Breaching through secrets,
    you asked
        if I ever wanted you.

Shouting through clouds of dust:
    My son, I wanted you
        before my own birth,

Before first sword cut to stone.

    Bathe in my tears, my blood.
    Know that I wanted you
        Before God.

Creating Zeus

Deep inside me—the whole pregnancy
he kicked: my fetus—a little boy
I did not know at the time

He reined my every thought
by just a slight twist and hiccup

Rest was anathema as he stirred and spiraled
amalgamating blood, bone, and flesh

A stretch of the arms ripped
the muscles down the center
of my belly—as he attempted
a herniated escape

With a kick to the ribs, his body
took over mine

As if I were a willing participant

Celestial Messenger

Did you guess?
    I am the angel
  with anthracite wings

flying above
    your honeycomb back
  near the Sinai Peninsula.

My heart was punctured
by three archers.

  Take the signals away
  clocks, scars, cigarettes.

They only make me bleed.

  Will you trade in the dead
at the used car dealer?

  My hero
  is perception.

To read a timepiece
in the darkness,

rough skin, thick fingers
  sharp nails,
  is a gift.

Harsh memories directed heavenward.

Witness

Jehovah declared me his child
His witness
Until I rejected him.

Now I am just
A broken woman
With memories that will not fade.

I offer prayers with no faith
That anyone hears them,

And I rail at a God
Who does not exist?
This is my testimony.

If I believed in any of it
Heaven, Hell, Paradise, Good,
Evil, I would be on my knees.

As it is, I stand on my feet
And believe that gravity
Holds me such that

Where I will always be
Is on the ground
Or in it.

Freedom from Speech

I graze my finger along your voice
where I see your deflated lips between greasy
brown globes.
After crushing the crowds
        of people, business men
pushing past you,

                you finally get

one argent coin
dancing in your dingy paper cup.

                I lived your life
on the margins of forgettable,
a chant, begging,
that satiates the borders around my society's
                              fractured song.

              On sight, I knew the feel
of the hand that took hold of you,

and I sense the eyes
so hot they burn you in winter's snow.

              After collecting scraps
from the bank's garbage,

        you mine for cans uptown
        to garner pennies on the bottle.

The gray, gum-splattered sidewalk carries a horde of minutes.

    Today, I count
    the people
    skipping past an empty casket.

A Petition for Unrecognized Children

Nation of various plump children
Can you pull our eyes?
Can you remove an owl from our nest?
And bleed the heartland…and our bowels?!

Our sickness against us…assimilation
or breaking us…mortality.
You shoot at our children…
You run down, you argue, How

Can cream clot the blood?

You scorn them, our children,
You are as you are, politicians.

Your tongue kills faster than bullets.
Bile will fill your craw.

If I accept you,
Gravel will clog my throat.

Believing you steals my loyalty from them.
Bowing to my knees,
The flaxen thread on my skin
Is a wound that won't heal

And a volcano and an orchid in my hands.

If my daughter dies in a shooting,
Do not bury her.
Lay her at the feet of those
Made from stone,

So that they may see their work.
If my son dies, raise him up
In place of the flag, so the world
Can see what we worship!
—And for the rest,

Leave the graves empty and
Pile the bodies before the throne.
Enjoin the corpses hand by hand
Across the Washington Mall.

You killed them, our children,
and you will kill more—before the sun sets

And pluck out our eyes
to spare us!

Sojourner

Truth is where I found you
In the cusp high over ultraviolet waves
Between your time as a slave and mine
Fighting off the results of bondage.

You were a woman who accepted no
Excuses for the lack of rights
For our mothers and daughters,
Demanded more for those who followed.

I am a woman who accepts that most
White men are fixed on one idea
As to how the world should be,
And it is on me to change their minds

Through words, or actions, but never
Through guns or swords, white bonnet
Wrapped on my head as I push
Away racial insults and profanity.

You never forgot to say who a woman
Could be, what a Black woman could do
When we eschewed weakness and misogyny.
No one helped you. You just carved the trail.

No one helps me either. That's what I learned
It means to be a Black woman.
To be strong, to plough, to plant, to raise barns.
That's what you did. I do that metaphorically.

Now, I raise children, plough through journals
With my pen. I always remember to never
Pin my tongue for fear of other's thoughts
This is the way you walked.

I try to get my half measure full,
But I think it is a little less
Difficult for me as it was
For you. Thank you for the
Quarter you earned.

It took us a long way, but
Today, the world is still
Turned upside down
And we are working
Hand by hand to

Flip it
Right side up

Donald Trump Is My Father

Despise his abundant grin,
Bristles extracting from his lips.

Despise his commonplace chin,
Jawlines disappearing into his neck.

Ingenious. From that instant, he will
        Forget his breathing. He is smoke

Divulged outside a crow's nest.
Despise his primitive morning's
Glance, your face, your breasts, you're

Gone now. Just a body. Despise
The city at peace, a contention of

Skyscrapers. Press for the rebellion.
Despise circuitry. I will not

Relinquish my hands, and the
Cogs will spit him out.

Detest his bitter speech: he
Pulls it from the drainpipe.

Detest his soul. I came disguised
Against thickets. Recoil from

The flag lodged in the old woman's
Chest. The baby tossed out of
Ice for her kisses to consciousness.

The man savaging his brain on opioids.
Recoil from the immigrant. A divided mirror

Capable of killing self-esteem.

A mind devoured. He has not
Begun. The centerpiece is dying

Away from the sun in a Harvest Box.

I Left Out "Bells and Whistles" Written with a Little Help from Websters Dictionary

The year I was born
was the same year
the term "assault weapon"
was born.

Assault weapon means any of various automatic or semiautomatic firearms.

Assault weapons could
have easily served
as pacifiers in my
South Central Los Angeles home.

I was seven the first time
I remember holding one.

Another phrase born with me is:

"Band-Aid" which means offering, making use of, or serving as a temporary or expedient remedy or solution.

Band-Aids which stuck
to my skin like pieces
of mismatched patchwork.
Band-Aids taught me the meaning
of flesh-toned.

When we didn't have Band-Aids,
we used tissue,
which is basically a poor Band-Aid.

Another term born with me is magnet school.
A "magnet school" is a school with superior facilities and staff and often a specialized curriculum designed to attract pupils from throughout a city or school district.

Magnet schools were initially a tool for desegregation.
I went to a gifted magnet school in Ladera Heights.
I was often teased for having old clothes.

Next birth phrase, "black-on-black"
meaning an altercation
involving a black person
against another black person.

Newscasters say things like
"Black-on-black crime plagues
our communities." Plague and black often
go together like "PCP" and
Sherman cigarettes which
also plagued black communities.
PCP means Phencyclidine a piperidine derivative $C17H25N$ used chiefly in the form of its hydrochloride especially as a veterinary anesthetic and sometimes illicitly as a psychedelic drug.

PCP was born with me.
I think my father picked
us up from the hospital at the same time.

Here's one that will surprise you: "Coronavirus," meaning any of a family of large single-stranded RNA viruses that have a lipid envelope studded with club-shaped spike proteins, infect birds and many mammals including humans, and include the causative agents of MERS, SARS, and COVID-19.

Blacks are five times more likely to die from coronavirus than whites. COVID-19 is also called the black plague.
Another birth word "delegitimize," which means to diminish or destroy the legitimacy, prestige, or authority of—

White people like to say that I'm
"playing the race card" to
delegitimize my argument.
"Delegitimize" is my twin, and
we are inseparable.

Russia delegitimizes the election.
All Lives Matter delegitimizes Black Lives Matter.
Confederate statues delegitimize racial struggles.
Voting law often delegitimizes the black vote.

Another word born with me is "SWAT" which means a police or military unit specially trained and equipped to handle unusually hazardous situations or missions.

SWAT officers are expert users of assault weapons.

SWAT broke into my backyard and obtained
access to my house to get a view of my white neighbor
who coincidentally was the voice of Bugs Bunny, Tazmanian
Devil and Mr. Magoo.

He held two women hostage with
an assault weapon.

He was back home by midnight.

Today SWAT used bean bags to kill a black man laying on the ground.
while his children watched.

SWAT delegitimized black life.
Authorities who allow abuse of power
delegitimize black life.

Laws that lack accountability
delegitimize black life.

My final birth phrase, "peace sign" meaning a sign made by holding the palm outward and forming a V with the index and middle fingers and used to indicate the desire for peace.

✌

Secrets

You stand in the dumpster beyond me.
Thin, scruffy, coffee mug on the lid beside you.

Empty bottles surround you. I stare
through the window—unnoticed by your eyes.

My body moves mechanically on the elliptical
as my heart beats out of step.

Sleepy cars swim slowly along the
misty asphalt. Wipers flick beads of dew.

Paint splotches your blue shirt like clouds
as you pick up a bottle with remnants of vodka

and pour it into your cup. You sip, relish
the taste and continue to separate

treasures from trash. In fifteen minutes
I dismount from the machine

with a vow to remember you, but
thoughts of you escape my mind until

the next time I climb onto the
elliptical. You, in a different shirt—wet

from the storm. Does the rain ever stop
the prisoner from escaping into the urn?

The machine pushes me towards the asbestos sky.
            We have seen too much.

A flower store next door advertises
                Two dozen roses—Twelve dollars

A Plea to the Inane

I call upon you frigid rain
        to build my inclination

toward the devastation of the doctrine.

Adoration will vibrate
        along a disfigured lattice

dropped from the rusted angle of lament.

I will keep on praying, always breaking
        silence against those sleeping.

My nerve is twined within the shell,
an instrument my creature
refuses to use.

You bathe me in petrol:
              incandescence.

You are me playing hide-and-seek
        inside kitchen cabinets.

I catechize you to chase goblins bubbling
        into wild wastelands.

Then I will eat gleaming gemstones
stripped from every cornice
of any false statue.

From that without exception, accept
every sincere prayer you did not return

from your shattered throne.

My Guardian Angel

When I take this pill, you must go.

Sanity leaves no room for you.

Remember the smell of biscuits,
scrambled eggs and sugar
syrup made by my mother
every morning after her beatings.

Look through the fog and cigarette smoke
at the fat, bloated corpse. He must be fed,

no matter how hungry you are.

Never talk back. He's stronger than you.

Angel, you abandoned me
just as Lot escaped Gomorrah.

When I am sane, you must deal with his ghost alone.

When you reach Hell, there will be millions of men
who beat their wives and raped their daughters.

You will recognize him by the old school shag afro,
big belly, gold chain, and the 'don't mess with Texas' belt buckle.

You and I will not play hopscotch or make daisy
chains for you tossed my childhood into the fire.

Now I toss you. Do not cry. He hates that.

I put this pill between my lips and swallow.

Phoenix

My spirit animal is the Phoenix.
She sits as a chick on the windowsill of my
Hospital room and grows, impatient—
Having burned to ash three days ago.

She toddles along the cement, against
The dark, cloudy Seattle skyline
Pecks at dead bugs, and waits
For the sunrise. Her feathers—

Black tufts of mists, sway with
The wind. When she can, she
Will leap from this sill and fly
And will likely burn to ash again.

She cannot stop herself from flying
Straight towards the sun.

Penance

I am memories
        wrapped in dark skin
absorbed by tissue and bone.

The notes I take serve as branded
relics of my tribulations.

Like a mural painted on quicksand
the mind cannot
        fix recollection.

When there is no palette with oils to mix,

When God recalls
        the art I choose to display without praise,

the whip's lash as steel-brushed strokes
across wrought iron flesh from fire,

learned from my parents,
in turn from their mammas and daddies,
handed down from the plantation,

what will I say?

This is my art.
        Inspired by God's flood.
                          His pestilence.

The bruises were his marks upon Cain
               the blood—the pain—upon Eve.

I will not ask forgiveness for denying him,

Just as He will not ask for mine.

I Stop Praying When I Learn You Abandoned Me

I shake my edges for the pretense
            of my prayers to you,

        for the cloud of hope alters
in a blustery air,

or it disappears in the mist
of the billowing

            skirt of sunset.

I pray at the time that breath
        prays for a tune

in contempt of meter
after hearing the cry
of a hundred runaway angels,

            up to the age I see feathers dwindle
            from your melting pedestal.

Centuries back, I sounded like a new
cherub blown from my base

            one solitary step
to block the cold.

        A lone comic sound fumed while
I pressed my knees in plaster
made from thistle and clover,

            along with your bare face
            which crushed against my sincerity.

I pray to your stopped ear
as a mute to the deaf,

to the vanishing fog
as it evaporates around me.

        Tell me,
what prayers have you heard?

           What bright pot of gold
can be credited to your virtues?

Against the morning moon
lay the rebuttal to my prayer,

    and lean over to face my eyes
    turned inside-out of the profit.

See the consequence of silence.

Blind yourself with the lack
    of right defense

as an abuser
who blames his wife.

While Dreaming of Harvey Weinstein

You peer at the top
      of my epidermal layers

in search of an opening
      I will never give you,

nor will I supplicate myself
to your playmate desires.

      With a wave of my hand

I misdirect your stare
      toward the honeyed chalice

resting beneath your hardened estuary.

Ice runs in sheaths
      providing millenary cracks

until you catch a glimpse of the
      twenty-four carat gargoyles

settling atop your head.

Yesterday, you ran free, devouring
      as ashes flew from your back,

a single conscious being

      before the small universe
      over which you presided.

Except the touch sharpened

just as I drenched my eyes with salt,
        vinegar and lye,

            and my mouth shrunk
            around you in disdain.

You grab my delicate tastes
        in the way that the grotesque

        captures the eye,
away from the listless arctic
while I congeal beyond you.

Tell me why
        I should drop to my knees?

When are the blazing mantles of fish
        to appear as blasphemy?

Into the editor's stomach
        bring your propositions
            just as concocted brilliance

erects to break away
        from your feet,

beyond the bounds of the plaster
concerning eternity.

Give away the flowering of abandonment.

Throw away the paralysis
    of uncertainty,

like a seraph powerless
    against God's daughters.

Yet Another Attempt at Self-Immolation

Have you decided to move backward
or forward today? You ask without
encouraging consonance.

A young disinterested mouse appears
approximately two seconds later
and dawdles along the New York Times

resting at my feet. We make eye contact and it
continues across the dark wood floor to the
kitchen island and climbs up the side like an

ebony spider. You did not notice the direction
of my eyes or the cake wrapper on the counter
crinkle as the mouse nibbles through.

What is it with you? You ask.
Why can't you just be happy?
Why can't you just suck it up?

The least attentive people find happiness

like the first potato chip, which was
made by mistake. Can you imagine
what it felt like to taste the first potato chip?

Every time I open a bag of Lays or Pringles,
I think, You're a mistake.
Truly a denizen on my thighs.

The abyss is not at one with the conscience.

It always avoids corruption.
None of these trivialities separate the cake.
What are you doing? You ask as I pick up the knife.
Slicing the cake, I respond.

Follow the crack pipe

Hold your breath as he
        exhales white smoke

Stop and wait—don't stare

Don't swallow the air
        he releases

If you breathe in
        you will see a ghost

Exhale himself with ether
        to the next circle

Run from the cloud which
        chokes within

        God has forgotten you
        in neon lights
        flashing against motel curtains

Cockroaches are fallen angels

The razor blade in your right palm
        plans have been made

One time he turned
        you into a seraph

Onc time he turned you into a demon

The tide rolls in
        you can wiggle your toes
        and feel bubbles on your skin

Stop for the final exhale
        a benediction

The divine moment

Remember the censer
that sinks into your stomach

No More Poems About My Father

It is the first day of the decade.
I walk my dog in the quiet syrupy Seattle air.
The Great Wheel flickers like a strobe light
against the morning night. It is as if the city
cannot stand the silence of anticipation.

Resolutions are waiting on the cusps of stale
champaign bubbles. Vows will be made, fulfilled,
or disappointed in rainy dreams while the population
sleeps off the night before. It was a bitter year's
close, along with wind, rain, and a lack of fireworks.

I spent the night without you. While you have
always been faithful, I wonder how long before
you are not. Because no matter the century, I
cannot help but believe that all men must be like
my father, who had to have every woman's mind,

which included mine pressed under his big toe.
Unfortunately, it is 17 lines into a new year, and as
I am sure Nostradamus would have predicted
if he had known the laughable irony of my existence,

I just broke my first resolution.

Partial Aphorism

Losing your mind is a hard
thing to accept.
It is easier to think
you lost your house keys.

Then there is a reasonable
excuse for the grasping
at your pockets.
The screams of frustration.

The anxiety. Of course
she broke through the front window.
She lost her house keys.
She cannot get into her house.

That is much easier to accept
than the cracked recesses of the brain.
When you are locked out of your mind
there is nowhere to go.
No understanding.

There is a chance you can
find your keys eventually.

But your mind? Who holds that key?

NYP Psychiatry

Lithium floats in the air.

Get security to escort women
       with suicidal tendencies

whose watery eyes are vacant from fear.

Stroke the gurney's back,
       the tenacious beast

who supports mania into the night.

       The treasury of impenetrable sanity
resides in a corn maze.

       The home of disinterest,
       I'm told,

is to think privately.

       This is where poltergeists embrace
the imagination, but reality resists.

Inform the seasoned chefs
of the anti-depressants, Duloxetine

       baking within the casserole.

Wait to see the blood
before taking the next slice.

To slash the menu
of my mind, to burn my dreams

I arrived a martyr
and exited a shadow.

After Landing in Lisbon

Becoming our own barren children
tourist clans magnify the customs lines.

Becoming our own confused apprentices
we exit. We are the daylight gleaming

against white tiles. Becoming the future
children climb cobblestone hills,

two steps at a time

while breathing, litered air. Becoming
a castle against blue sky, marble stones

etch the horizon becoming
a puzzle. The past hides

our present thoughts, but we will find
our future. In respect of statues

we bow to them.

In respect of the fountains, they
kiss our cheeks. In respect of the

buildings falling apart,

the earth shook long ago
by the bonfire in its center.

The god swaddling his favorite angel screamed.

In respect of the stairways
a harsh climb is incapable of

reaching heaven's hem.

In Fado music, all hope is done.
The fish are often swimming

along the smile of the shore.

Quintessential Pirate

I sail archetypal waters
the moment I find my tune.

My fathers crossed the Norwegian Sea
in trade ships as vikings.

My mothers crossed the Gulf of Guinea
in trade ships as slaves.

Across the Atlantic, as the bogey croons
swam the creator of song.

I cross the Mississippi and touch the Pacific,
the songs of my mother.

I sang in Norway
       a year ago.
Blanched people.
Unrecognizable tunes.

       When young,
            I sang Rapper's Delight
            on 111th and Prairie.

The lights flash strangely farther
across my dancing eyes.

Oiled vocal chords
flow dark along the sand.

I Am the Complete Secret

(Scandinavia 820–1863 A.D.)

The glacier is a beast who resides in a question mark.

My DNA
deceives my skin.

My Norway
is buried under
Southern shadows.

There are no stories
of Olaf, Halcon.

The Northern lights blind the history
written by the slave trader
who carried the bills of lading.

In Oslo, I saw
the Oseburg
that failed to cross the sea to meet me.

In 1001 when
they discovered home,

did they imagine
me in chains?

The orca tear through the sea
while I tread water.

I had parents but lived as an orphan.

Let the results
reveal my blood
and the stain I hide.

Censorship

My poems die at the root
at stem and bloom.
I could carry them to mass on
tops of wreaths and sing funeral lullabies.

My memories circle as melodies
around the same place, a face

That does not escape because
it hides in my eyes. I bite
it between my lips, and
I breathe it within my lungs.

I am its mirror, its reincarnation
The lines, the rhymes,
make another circle

back to the cloak, back
to the demon that encapsulates
nightmares. It is my face

long dead, it resurrects
itself in my belly, again
and again. It turns around.

I wish I could call it ugly
but beauty resides with
those who hold it within their
hands.

My fingers were chopped off at birth
so I cannot touch the petal or
the thorn. My eyes were

plucked free by roosters
with long red combs and plumes
But they still call me beautiful
As they mount the hills

of my blind sided haunch.
This affectation is for the
lost words, the runaway

letters. The gagged voice.

ogue

I feel my color burn
    in the belly of my t.v.

I digest the waving Confederate flags
    of unburdened arms.

I am all set to combust
    into shout,
        into chant, rallying cry.

    Declaration weaved from ancestral blood.

In the turn of a swastika,
I taste yesterday
    on my tongue.

They lynch the venerated rope around my neck.

The President burns a cross
    on my lawn
        with his derision.

Through statues, highways, ships,
    memorials of the Confederacy,
they deface the memory of a country
    who repeatedly attempts to expel me.

About the Author

Katerina Canyon was born and raised in Los Angeles, California. She is a 2019 and 2020 Pushcart Prize nominee. She served as the Sunland-Tujunga California Poet Laureate from 2001 to 2004. During that time, she started and ran the Shouting Coyote Poetry Festival, and she traveled the country promoting poetry and poetry events. Her work has been published in publications such as *Meniscus, New York Times,* and *Huffington Post* United States and Germany. She was a Heartland Review finalist. She is an independent poetry workshop teacher in Seattle, Washington.

www.ingramcontent.com/pod-product-compliance
Lightning Source LLC
Chambersburg PA
CBHW032237080426
42735CB00008B/890

This is my time to sing,
    a claim from on high

        as words skitter
            across the page.